THE INFORMATION REVOLUTION

Stephanie Kraus

Consultant

Jennifer M. Lopez, NBCT, M.S.Ed.
Teacher Specialist—History/Social Studies
Office of Curriculum & Instruction
Norfolk Public Schools

Publishing Credits

Rachelle Cracchiolo, M.S.Ed., *Publisher*
Conni Medina, M.A.Ed., *Editor in Chief*
Emily R. Smith, M.A.Ed., *Content Director*
Véronique Bos, *Creative Director*
Robin Erickson, *Art Director*
Michelle Jovin, M.A., *Associate Editor*
Lee Aucoin, *Senior Graphic Designer*

Image Credits: front cover, p.1 Frank Martin/BIPs/Getty Images; p.5 (top) Internet Archive; p.5 (bottom) Paul Coulomb; p.6 Windell Oskay/Flickr; p.7 (all) U.S. Army; p.8 AlisonW; p.9 Thomas Nguyen; p.10 (right) NASA; p.11 Bettmann/Getty Images; p.12 (both) Andrew "FastLizard4" Adams; p.13 (left) Jay L. Clendenin/Los Angeles Times via Getty Images; p.14 (left) Roberto Brosan, George Segal (sculpture) for TIME; p.14 (right) secretlondon123/Flickr; p.16 (left) Museum of Applied Arts & Sciences, Australia; pp.16?17 Sal Veder/AP Photo; p.17 (right) Raneko/Flickr; p.18 Julie Deshaies/Shutterstock; p.19 (top) Doug Wilson/Corbis via Getty Images; p.19 (bottom) Ruben de Rijcke; p.20 CERN/Science Source; p.21 (right) Tim Berners-Lee for CERN; p.22 (left) FPS/Newscom; p.22 (right) Tom Kelley Archive/iStock; p.23 Feature Photo Service/Newscom; p.25 MailHamdi/Shutterstock; p.28 Ken Wolter/Shutterstock; p.32 (right) Casimiro PT/Shutterstock; all other images from iStock and/or Shutterstock.

Library of Congress Cataloging-in-Publication Data

Names: Kraus, Stephanie, author.
Title: The information revolution / Stephanie Kraus.
Description: First edition. | Huntington Beach : Teacher Created Materials, 2019. | Includes index. | Audience: Ages 7. | Audience: Grades 2-3. | Summary: "Today, it's hard to imagine life without smartphones and the internet. But those technologies weren't around 50 years ago. Between 1950 and 2001, the development of technology changed the world. Not only did it revolutionize the way humans communicate and share information, it changed the world's economy. This time became known as the Information Revolution"-- Provided by publisher.
Identifiers: LCCN 2019024412 (print) | LCCN 2019024413 (ebook) | ISBN 9781425850777 (paperback) | ISBN 9781425850777 (ebook)
Subjects: LCSH: Telecommunication--History--Juvenile literature. | Information technology--History--Juvenile literature.
Classification: LCC TK5102.2 .K73 2019 (print) | LCC TK5102.2 (ebook) | DDC 303.48/33--dc23
LC record available at https://lccn.loc.gov/2019024412
LC ebook record available at https://lccn.loc.gov/2019024413

TCM Teacher Created Materials
5301 Oceanus Drive
Huntington Beach, CA 92649-1030
www.tcmpub.com
ISBN 978-1-4258-5077-7

Printed by: 51497
Printed in: China

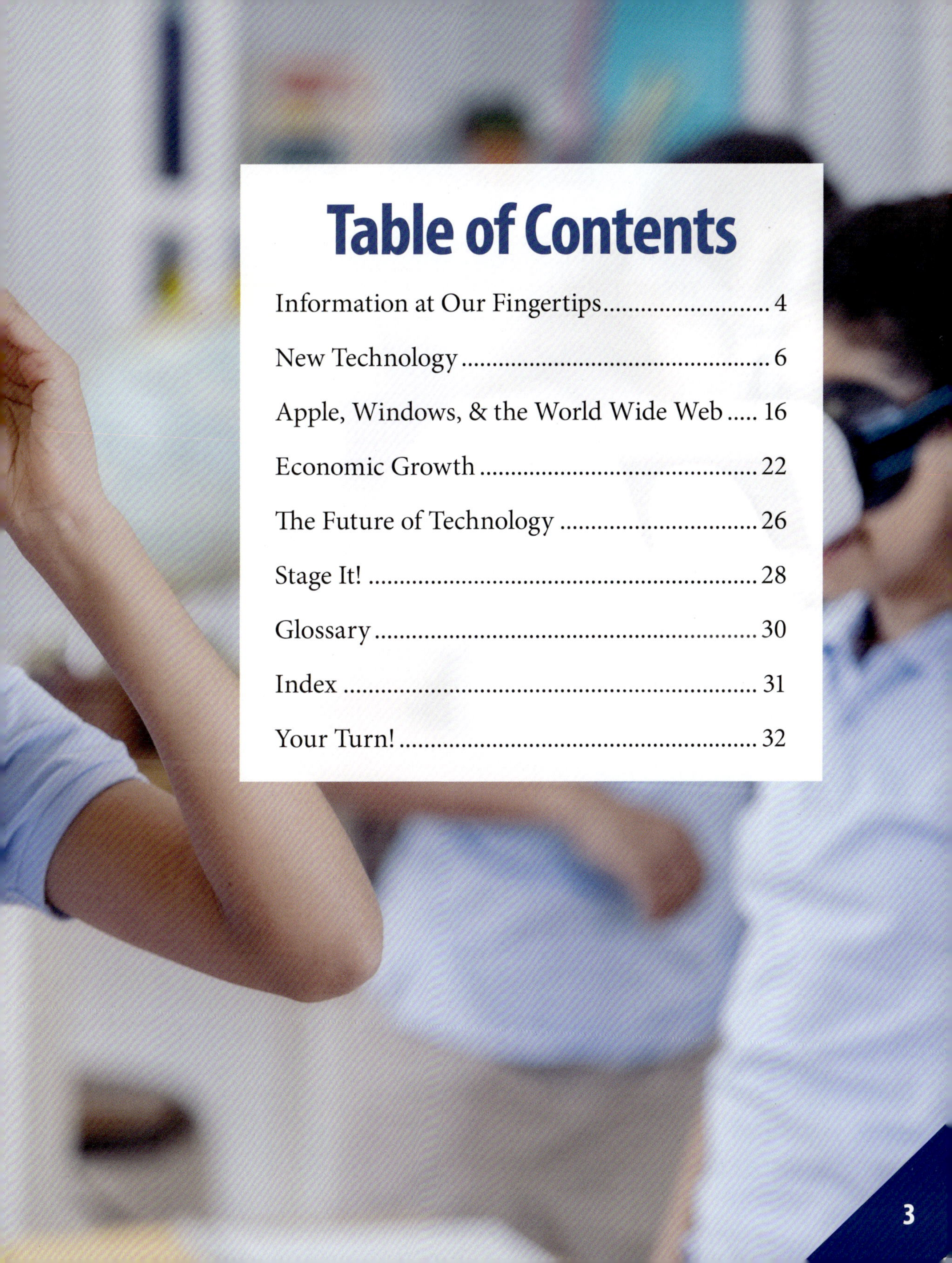

Table of Contents

Information at Our Fingertips

When was the last time you *googled* something? Did you know that term didn't mean anything 20 years ago? Today, it's pretty common. It means we are able to look up the answer to any question we have. All we have to do is go online. It wasn't always this easy.

The first fully functional digital computer was invented in 1946. Yet, home computers did not show up for another 30 years. Soon after, the internet took the world by storm. People could have information at their fingertips. Then, emails started being sent around the world. Instead of sending a letter that would arrive in days or weeks, people could write emails that arrived in seconds. People could buy and sell goods easier and faster than ever before. These things helped the world economy grow. New technologies were created each year. Companies raced to come up with new ideas first. The competition meant that companies had to make things better, faster, and cheaper than everyone else.

Suddenly, people were getting information like never before. People came up with a name for this era—the Information Revolution.

◀ People can have digital doctors' appointments.

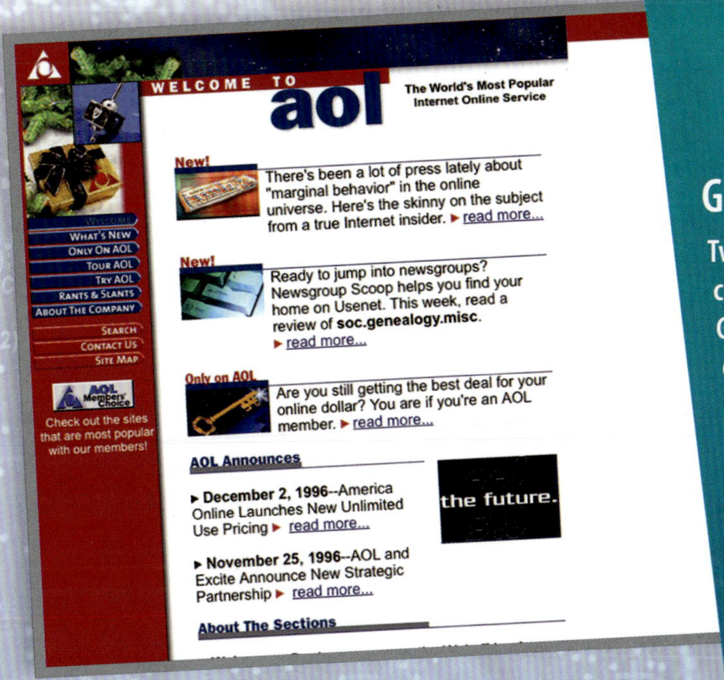

America Online® homepage in 1996

America Online® homepage in 2019

Google It!

Two Stanford University students created Google™ in 1998. The name Google is a play on the word *googol*. *Googol* is a mathematical term that represents the numeral 1 followed by 100 zeros. The students chose this name to show how much information the internet could hold.

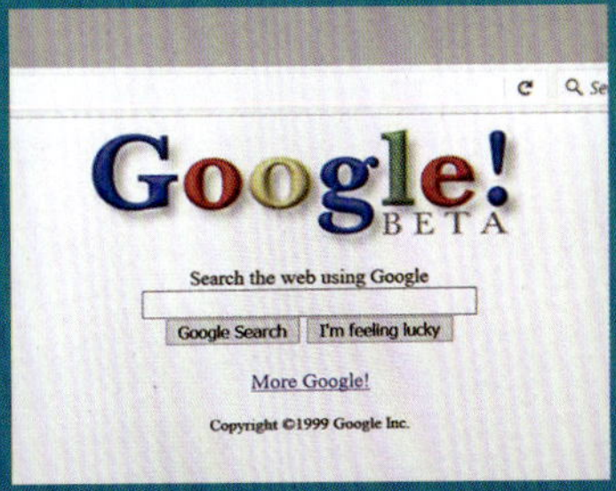

Faster Connections

Access to the internet has greatly sped up since its introduction. If someone wanted to download a 2-hour movie today, it could take up to 30 minutes. In the early days of the internet, it could take about 213 hours (almost 9 days)!

New Technology

Television Tubes

Televisions called CRTs also use vacuum tubes. In the 1960s, 9 out of 10 American households owned a CRT television set. However, LCD televisions started to slowly take over the market in the early 2000s. In 2007, LCD televisions outsold CRT televisions for the first time. Now, the old "tube TVs" can be hard to find.

Hard Day's Work

To make the ENIAC work, people had to manually plug and unplug wires by hand. It took several days to reset the machine for a new program.

One of the first digital computers was built in Pennsylvania in 1946. It was called the ENIAC. It was a huge machine that could fill a room. The ENIAC had 40 panels. Each panel was about 2 feet (0.5 meters) wide, 2 feet (0.5 meters) deep, and 8 feet (2.5 meters) tall! It cost $400,000. The ENIAC used 18,000 glass vacuum tubes to control its **electrical current**. To extend the life of the tubes, the machine was rarely turned off. Those long hours of operation meant the tubes used a lot of power and gave off a lot of heat.

The ENIAC was a marvel for its time. But, all those big vacuum tubes made the machine massive. People wanted smaller computers. So in 1947, three scientists at Bell Labs performed an experiment. They built a small device using gold and a crystal. Then, they added electricity to the device. The scientists could use the device to increase or switch electrical signals. These scientists had created the first **transistor**. It was smaller and used much less power than vacuum tubes did. It was first used for calculators. But it was soon being used in almost all electronics.

◀ 1947 Bell Labs transistor

▲ The ENIAC was primarily used by the U.S. Army.

▲ A worker plugs wires into the ENIAC computer.

Small and Powerful

In the years after the invention of the transistor, more and more computers were made. But they were still large and costly. It wasn't until 1965 that the first desktop computer was sold to the public. It was called the Programma 101. It was a large calculator that ran basic math problems. The Programma 101 was shown at the World's Fair in the year before its release. The crowds were amazed. They could not believe a fully working computer could fit on a single desk. And it weighed less than 100 pounds (45 kilograms)! Compared with other computers at the time, it was easy to use. It sold for $3,200—just slightly less than the average cost of a new car at that time.

▲ Programma 101

Near the same time, engineers were working to make computer **circuits** smaller. In 1971, the tech company Intel® created its first **microprocessor**. It was called the Intel 4004. The tiny chip would act as a computer's "brain." The chip was small enough to fit inside calculators and music players.

Orders for the new **silicon** chip poured in. It sparked many new businesses in Northern California. This area came to be known as Silicon Valley. There, the race was on to make smaller chips that could do even more.

Calculator or Computer

Italian engineer Pier Giorgio Perotto created the Programma 101. In 1967, Hewlett-Packard® (HP) used his design to create a new computer. But HP called its device a "portable calculator." This was meant to help with sales since many people were not comfortable with computers at that time.

Other Uses for Chips

Many television sets use microprocessor chips. The chips make images clearer as well as making them seem more realistic. "Smart TVs" (television sets that can connect to the internet) also use chips to load apps and stream media. The better the microprocessor, the faster apps will load and the clearer images will be.

◀ The Intel 4004 microprocessor was about the size of a pinkie nail.

enlarged by about 650%

Space Exploration

In 1957, scientists in the Soviet Union launched the world's first satellite into space. It was called *Sputnik 1*. People in the U.S. government were worried. They were scared of what the Soviet Union would do next. The next year, the U.S. government formed the National Aeronautics and Space Administration (NASA). NASA scientists quickly launched the *Explorer 1* satellite. In 1961, Soviet scientists did one better. They sent the first human into space.

One Small Step

Neil Armstrong and Edwin "Buzz" Aldrin were the first astronauts to walk on the moon. As Armstrong set foot on the moon, he spoke his now-famous phrase: "One small step for man, one giant leap for mankind."

Impressive Results

Astronauts were able to type simple commands to control the spacecraft. The computers used in the *Apollo 11* landing were less powerful than smartphones are today. But, they were still able to land the team safely on the moon and get them home.

▲ An unmanned spacecraft—*Ranger 9*—broadcasts images of the moon's surface in 1965.

During this time, the United States and the Soviet Union did not have a good relationship. This time was called the Cold War. The "Space Race" was one part of it. U.S. leaders knew they needed to do more to win. NASA bought at least 10 Programma 101s. It sent one on its *Apollo 11* moon landing in 1969.

At the time, many people in the United States had just bought their first television sets. People gathered around their TVs to watch the moon landing. About 600 million people watched the event. It was a huge moment in U.S. history.

Apollo 11 astronauts Neil Armstrong, Michael Collins, and Buzz Aldrin

The Internet

During the Cold War, the U.S. military looked for a better way to communicate around the world. Some people were worried phone **networks** would be wiped out in an attack. They wanted to make sure lines of communication would still be open. Some people thought the United States needed a better way to share information with other countries. Researchers came up with an idea that would solve both issues. They worked on linking computers together in a network to share information. There would be no "central hub" that an enemy could destroy. Even if parts were damaged, the rest would still work.

Scientists at the U.S. Department of Defense created a system called ARPANET. Two scientists sent the first message in 1969. The scientists typed two letters before it crashed. The two letters were *L* and *O*. (They were the first two letters of LOGIN.) Over time, researchers created a grid of networks. This allowed computers to send, receive, and pass information between them. It was later called the *internet*.

This computer was the first to be connected to ARPANET.

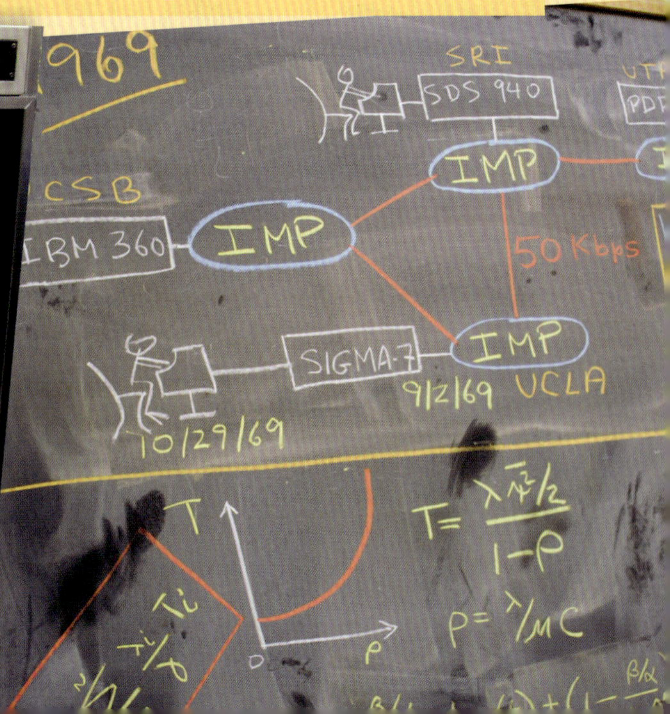

One of ARPANET's founders stands by the machine that helped connect computers to the ARPANET network.

The Name Game

The term *internet* was first used in 1974. No one is sure who first used the term. But *internet* came out of a shortening of the term *internetworking*.

Computer Concerns

Many television shows in the 1960s focused on computers and space travel. Shows such as *Star Trek*, *Lost in Space*, and *The Jetsons* were all popular in their time. In these shows, computers often help make life easier and safer. These shows played a role in changing public concerns about computers.

Dialing Up

Early on, only some people could use the internet. You either had to be part of the military or part of a research group. But the U.S. government saw that the internet was growing. In 1991, they chose to open the network up to the public.

The internet was open to everyone, but people needed a phone line to connect. Phone lines could only carry a small amount of data. This meant connecting was slow. Companies began selling dial-up **modems**. These modems changed digital information to **analog**. That was needed for data to

▲ Early internet users placed their telephones into cradles like this to connect to the internet.

Games at Home

The first home video console was sold in 1972. It was called the Magnavox Odyssey. The Odyssey was not very successful. That was due, in part, to the mistaken belief that the Odyssey could only be played on Magnavox TV sets. Regardless, the Odyssey paved the way for the home video game industry to follow.

A Big Year

In 1983, *TIME* magazine named the personal computer the "Machine of the Year." The main writer on the project finished his work on a typewriter. But, *TIME*'s newsroom upgraded to word processors within the same year.

be able to travel along phone lines. Soon after, **fiber-optic** cables were created. They let more information travel every minute. Download speeds were now 10–20 times faster than they had been.

There was still one question on a lot of people's minds: Who owned the internet? The answer was the same then as it is now—no one. Since there was no owner, many people weren't sure about trusting the network. There was a lot of private information being put on the internet. Military experts were worried. They thought other countries might steal information. They wanted it to be spy-proof. Some universities wanted the internet to be used for research only. Still, the internet kept growing.

▼ fiber-optic cables

Apple, Windows, & the World Wide Web

In late 1974, an engineer named Ed Roberts built a small computer kit. It was called the Altair 8800. The kit sold for $397. Only skilled engineers could build the computer, but it was still a hit.

At the same time, two friends—Steve Wozniak and Steve Jobs—were testing computers. They worked in their parents' garages. Wozniak worked off Roberts's design. Wozniak wanted to create a personal computer. So, Wozniak and Jobs launched their own company in 1976. They called it Apple®. First, they made a desktop computer called the Apple I. It was not like computers today. It was basically just a **circuit board**. People still needed to buy a monitor, keyboard, and case.

first Apple I computer

The next year, Apple released the Apple II. It came with both **hardware** and **software**. The Apple II showed colors on its screen. Apple created a new logo with a striped rainbow to advertise its color screens.

Customers loved the Apple II. Within five years of its release, Apple had made $583 million in sales. They came out with the first Macintosh in 1984. It was a bulky, desktop computer.

▼ Jobs, Sculley, and Wozniak unveil an Apple computer in 1984.

Coming Back

In 1985, an Apple executive named John Sculley fired Steve Jobs. Sculley thought Jobs took too long to correct some of the problems Apple had with its Macintosh computers. Jobs started another project called NeXT, which was later bought by Apple. So, in 1996, Jobs found himself back at the company he had helped to create.

Take Your TV with You

While Apple was taking the computer world by storm, the TV industry was growing too. In 1983, a new type of TV (called LCD) was invented. LCD televisions were much lighter and thinner. Portable TVs were now possible. The screens on these TVs were often only a couple of inches wide!

Windows Meets World

Apple's hardware was hugely popular. But childhood friends Bill Gates and Paul Allen knew more could be done with the software. During their college years, they started working on software. In 1976, they founded a company called Microsoft®. Gates and Allen created an **operating system**. It was called MS-DOS. They also created a **graphical user interface** (GUI), which would later be called Windows®. The GUI let users put in commands by clicking a mouse on a symbol, instead of typing in **code**. Now, anyone could use computers.

In the 1980s, Microsoft made another smart move. Computer company IBM® asked to buy Windows. Instead, Microsoft partnered with IBM. This meant every IBM computer sold would have Windows on it. IBM paid Microsoft for every computer sold.

Microsoft Office® was released in 1989. It helped people create documents, spreadsheets, slideshows, and more. The software changed how work was done. Microsoft sales soared.

Microsoft soon had control of most of the world's personal-computer market. Gates and Allen were both billionaires. People were inspired by their success. Some people worked to start their own technology businesses.

Home Gaming

In 2001, Microsoft introduced Xbox®—its first home gaming console on the market. Microsoft also released the popular video game Halo®. The success of Halo helped drive the success of the Xbox. Now, Xbox is one of the most popular home-gaming consoles on the market. Over one hundred million Xbox consoles have been sold since its release.

Giving Back

Around 10,000 of the early Microsoft employees became millionaires. With his new wealth, Gates wanted to give back. He started a charity called the Bill & Melinda Gates Foundation. It aims to improve global health care and reduce poverty.

Microsoft cofounders Gates and Allen work in 1984.

This IBM computer was the first to come with MS-DOS.

The World Wide Web

In 1989, computer scientist Tim Berners-Lee began work on a new project. He called it the World Wide Web. It was a way for networked computers to exchange information. These new web pages looked very bare and simple compared to today. But they were still revolutionary for the time.

At the same time, Berners-Lee also built two other systems. One system was called *hypertext markup language*, or HTML. HTML is a way of formatting text, images, and audio on web pages. Berners-Lee's second system was a web browser. A *browser* is a type of software that lets computers find and display web pages.

Berners-Lee demonstrates his World Wide Web project in 1994.

All three systems work together to give people access to the World Wide Web. First, a user opens a browser on a computer, phone, tablet, or other device. Then, they can type in the **URL** for the web page they wish to visit. Their computer sends a request to the web page. The web page's **servers** send back a response. That response comes in the form of HTML. The browser reads and displays the HTML for the user. All of that happens in just a couple of seconds!

▼ A student learns basic HTML coding.

The Internet vs. the Web

The *internet* is the system of networks that connects computers together. The World Wide Web is how people access information on the internet. Most web pages begin with "www." That stands for World Wide Web.

Rise of Web Browsers

In 1991, Berners-Lee released his browser. It was called WorldWideWeb. Two years later, a new browser called Mosaic was released. It offered users the ability to "point-and-click." It could also show both text and images on a single page. People loved Mosaic. Over the next few years, companies raced one another to create more-advanced browsers.

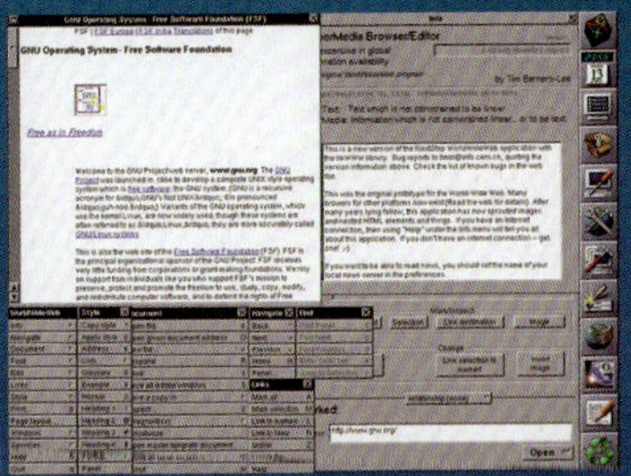

Economic Growth

Companies started to see the potential of the World Wide Web. They hired people to make websites. The sites could promote their brands and sell products or services. Websites help people shop quickly instead of driving from store to store. With just a few clicks, people can buy concert tickets, airline tickets, or reserve hotel rooms. Buying goods or services online is called *electronic commerce*, or *e-commerce*. Today, it's hard to picture life without it.

▼ A customer uses an ATM in 1972.

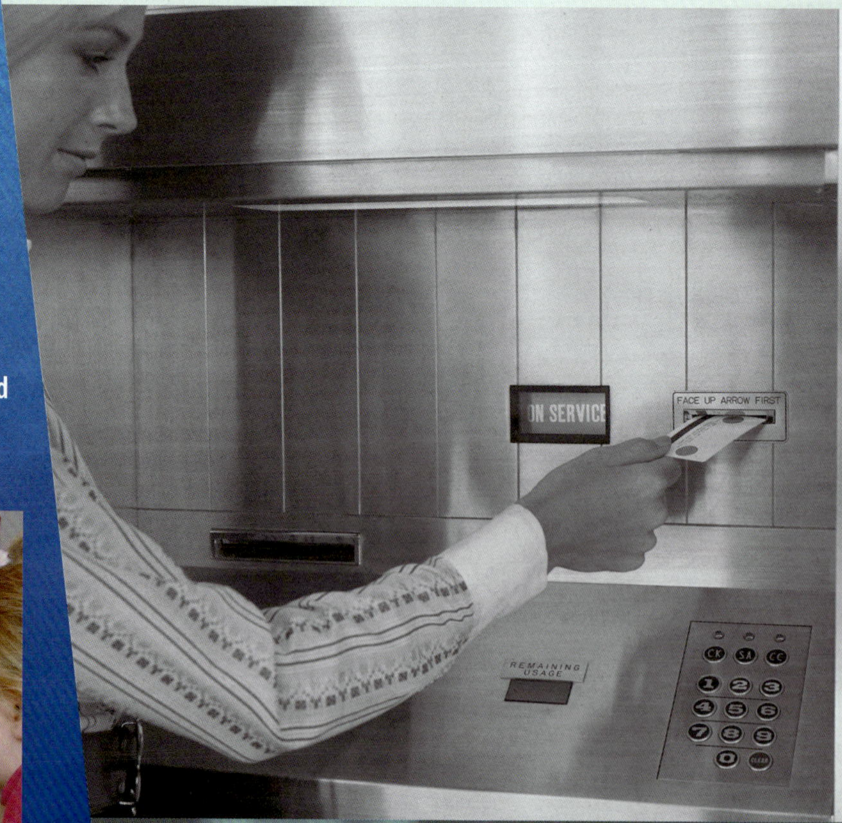

Help Wanted

The birth of the internet created new jobs in the technology industry. People could work as web developers, video game designers, online marketers, and advertisers. Through the years, even more jobs have come out of the internet, such as social media managers and influencers.

Interest in the Internet

Television shows largely ignored the internet in the 1990s. Some popular shows of the time, such as *The X-Files* and *Friends*, only mentioned the internet as horror stories or as jokes. It wasn't until the early 2000s that TV shows used the internet as a helpful tool.

Businesses that **invested** in the internet and in computers were saving money. For instance, think of an ATM. People can use ATMs at any time of day or night. Bank owners can hire fewer employees if computers do the work for them. Even if computers were expensive, businesses would make the money back.

Computers also created more high-paying jobs. Large companies were hiring people for technology jobs. The United States created 18 million jobs in the 1990s. The **unemployment rate** went down. It was the lowest it had been in 30 years.

▼ **Students learn how to use computers in 1999.**

The Growth of Cable Television

Economic growth expanded beyond the World Wide Web. Many companies were making their mark in television at this time. By the end of the 1980s, cable television was growing. It was quickly becoming a way to make a lot of money. Before cable, Americans did not have many TV options. There were three major TV channels that people could watch—NBC, CBS, and ABC. All three of those channels had begun as radio channels. People had known these names for decades.

As cable TV began to spread throughout the country, companies created new channels. Slowly, the "Big Three" were losing viewers. Television channels also became more focused. The Big Three had always hosted a wide range of shows. That way, they could appeal to many viewers. New cable channels began targeting certain types of viewers. There were channels with only cooking shows. Other channels played home-improvement shows. Still other channels had all-day sports shows. Cable TV had something for everyone.

People were thrilled with the options they had. Americans began watching more and more TV. Soon, a "24-hour news cycle" formed. People had access to news at all times. With the help of the internet, news spread. People were getting information faster than ever.

More than half of Americans subscribe to at least one streaming service.

Over the Years

Cable TV was introduced in the 1940s. However, people did not see why they should pay for cable when the Big Three were free. As cable channels offered more content, people made the switch. In 1970, about 1 in 12 American households had cable TV. Within 10 years, it had gone up to almost 1 in 4 households. In recent years, streaming services, such as Netflix®, have begun to take over as many Americans' preferred method of watching TV.

Senator Kennedy

In 1968, Senator Robert Kennedy was shot and killed. The murder was shown live over multiple major news networks. Kennedy's death occurred just two months after civil rights leader Martin Luther King Jr. had been killed. The **riots** that followed King's murder were broadcast on national TV. In the days after Kennedy's death, stations offered more than 140 hours of coverage. This was the first instance of the 24-hour news cycle.

The Future of Technology

Adults & Screens

In the United States, the average adult spends about 11 hours every day interacting with media. That breaks down to about 5 hours of watching TV, 2 hours of being on a phone, 2 hours of listening to the radio, and 2 hours of other tasks.

Teens & Screens

In the United States, the average teenager spends about 9 hours every day interacting with media. Almost 7 of those hours are spent looking at screens. Some schools now celebrate Screen Free Week to encourage teens to take a break from electronics.

Technology has changed the way we live. In schools, teachers may use tablets instead of textbooks to teach lessons. Hundreds of billions of emails are sent each day. At home, people use devices for entertainment. People can stream TV shows and films from their couches. Social media helps people share highlights from their days. People hear about news faster than ever, and there is an app for almost everything.

So, what's next? No one can know for sure. But, it is safe to say the future holds smarter technology and smarter users. Companies have cars that drive themselves. Virtual reality is

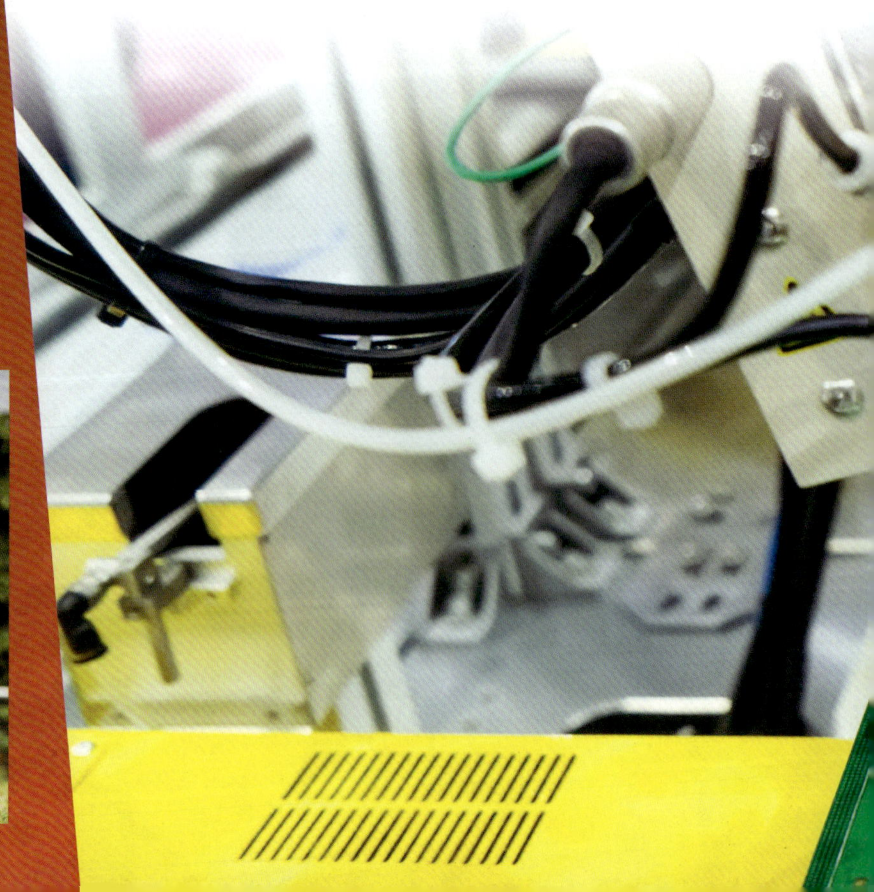

changing entertainment and making its way into schools. Space travel is safer and more advanced than ever. Robots are becoming smarter, and people are becoming better at interacting with them. And 3-D printing is helping the medical and manufacturing fields.

Every generation will look more and more different from yours. The future will see devices and technology that have never been imagined. What do you see in your future? Start experimenting now. You may lead the next Information Revolution!

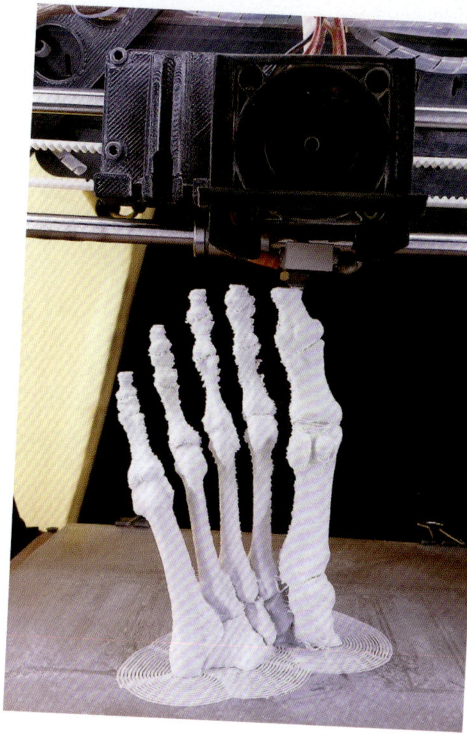

▲ 3-D printed foot

◀ A robot assembles microchips.

Stage It!

The Information Revolution was a time of rapid change. People were experimenting with new devices and crafting new technologies every year. It was an exciting time for many people.

Write a play that shows the changes in technology during the Information Revolution. Make sure to include key figures, such as Steve Wozniak, Bill Gates, and Tim Berners-Lee. Include important companies and institutions, such as Microsoft, ABC, NASA, and the U.S. government. End your script with future inventions that we've never heard of!

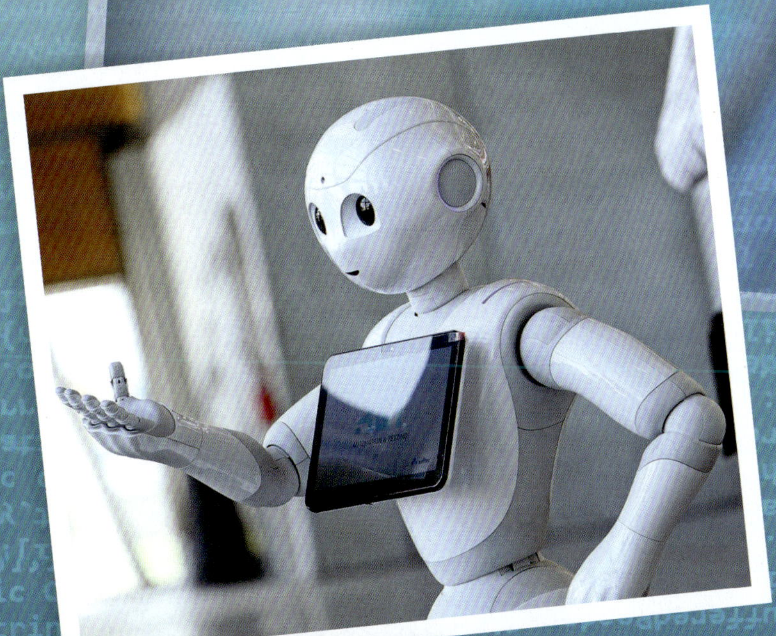

Glossary

analog—a way of transmitting data by using electronic pulses

circuit board—a flat piece that has many electrical circuits and is used in electrical equipment

circuits—electrical components that contain complete electrical currents

code—a set of instructions for a computer

electrical current—a complete flow of electricity

fiber-optic—thin threads that carry information in the form of light signals

graphical user interface—a program that allows someone to use a mouse to click on icons when using a computer

hardware—computer equipment, including circuit boards, fans, power supplies, and more

invested—used money to purchase stock, property, or other things in order to make more money

microprocessor—a device that controls information and what a computer does

modems—devices that change signals from one form to another

networks—systems of computers and devices that are connected to each other

operating system—the main program in a computer that controls how a computer works

riots—public disturbances

servers—the main computers in networks which provide services and files to other computers

silicon—made of a chemical element and used in computers and electronics

software—the programs that run on computer equipment and perform certain actions

transistor—a small device that controls the flow of electricity in electronic devices

unemployment rate—the total number of people in a place who are looking for jobs but have not been hired yet

URL—abbreviation for Uniform Resource Locator; the symbols and letters that stand for a web page's address

Index

Your Turn!

The Information Revolution changed the way people thought of and interacted with technology. Television shows informed public opinions about what was happening in the world. The internet provided fast, convenient access to information like never before. Some people feared what these new machines would be capable of doing.

Today, most American households have television sets and internet connections. From streaming movies and television shows to internet-based video games, television and the internet work together to create an interconnected experience.

Imagine you work in the technology industry in the 1960s. You know that people are nervous about the new computers that are coming to the market. Design an advertisement to tell people how computers can make their lives easier. Your advertisement can have any format you want—a poster, a newspaper ad, a radio ad, or anything else! Then, show your advertisement to friends and see if it would have persuaded them to buy computers.